TWISTED TONGUES

Jokes, Comics, Facts, and Tongue Twisters

By Kit Lively and David Lewman

Illustrated by David DeGrand

• • •

Workman Publishing ✳ New York

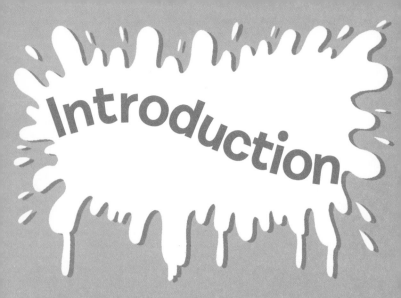

Introduction

"She sells seashells by the seashore."

No, you didn't accidentally pick up a book about a beach gift shop. That sentence up there is what's known as a "tongue twister." Try to say it ten times fast (go ahead!) and you are almost guaranteed to mix up the "sh" and "s" sounds. That's part of the fun of tongue twisters; they make us confuse similar sounds and the result is "twisted"—as in "see sells sheshells by the sheasore," or worse.

This is a book of tongue twisters, but it has a bonus factor. All the tongue twisters here are gross. Some are just a little bit gross; some are *very* gross. In this book, instead of twisting your tongue around a sentence about someone selling shells (*yawn!*), you'll be trying to say, "Big bedbugs bite pet pugs' butts." (*Pardon me, did you say "butts"?*)

For maximum enjoyment of this book, follow these steps:

Twist Level 6

1. Find a gross tongue twister you want to try. You can refer to the Twist Level meters throughout—they rate each tongue twister's difficulty on a scale from one to ten.

2. Now say the tongue twister ten times fast. Don't let yourself pause or slow down!

3. Get someone else in on the act—you can take turns with friends or family, trying out twisters of different difficulties and even challenging one another using some of the book's contests and competitions.

4. Did you mess up a lot? Were you repulsed by the grossness? Were you kicked off the school bus? All of those things are possible, and any of them means that this book is working.

When you want to take a break from exercising your tongue, lips, and mouth, there are also revolting facts to read (like the one on page 90 about the leech that lived in a woman's nose) and information about how and why tongue twisters happen. To top it all off, there are dozens of gross riddles and jokes told by these two talking boogers:

Now get twisting!

Bigger Booger   Baby Booger

And maybe keep a barf bag handy just in case.

Library of Congress Cataloging-in-Publication Data is available.

ISBN: 978-1-5235-1016-0

Design by Claire Torres
Cover design by John Passineau
Illustration by David DeGrand

Workman books are available at special discounts when purchased in
bulk for premiums and sales promotions as well as for fund-raising or
educational use. Special editions or book excerpts can also be created
to specification. For details, contact the Special Sales Director at the
address below or send an email to specialmarkets@workman.com.

Workman Publishing Co., Inc.
225 Varick Street
New York, NY 10014-4381

workman.com

WORKMAN is a registered trademark of
Workman Publishing Co., Inc.

Printed in China

First printing September 2020

10 9 8 7 6 5 4 3 2 1

PART 1:
CRUSTY CRITTERS
AND
GREASY CREATURES

Please release the leech's leash.

Giraffes clean out their nostrils with their tongues.

WHY PICK WHEN YOU CAN LICK?

Male hippos fling their poop by twirling their tails. They do this to mark their territories and attract the attention of females.

UM . . . MAYBE TRY FLOWERS?

Blobby Bobby gobbled gobs of soggy doggies.

Herb heard a sick squirrel hurl.

No, I do not, Bigger Booger. Goodbye.

But boogers always stick together!

Mollie's mollusk makes musky mucus.

Brad's beasts breathe bad breath best.

Some dung beetles have special mouthparts that they use to eat dung.

BUT THEY'RE STILL LOUSY KISSERS.

The **skink** thinks the **skunk** stinks.

The skunk thunk the skink stunk.

Twisted Challenges

Find a hard tongue twister from this book. Then try it . . .

... while doing jumping jacks.

... while trying to touch your nose with your tongue.

... with your lips closed.

... underwater.

... to the tune of a parent's least
favorite song.

... while sipping a glass of water.*

... without closing your lips.

... saying it backward.

... with your teeth clenched.

... while eating crackers.*

... after you've had a filling at the
dentist.

*You may be asked to clean up.

Annie's
anemone*
is Emmy's
enemy.

*Pronounced "a-NEH-meh-ne"

An immobile, column-shaped sea animal with wavy
tentacles that resembles a plant or flower.

Jim's jam jar of squirming germy worms.

Did you hear about the genius snail?

Um, what about him?

He was way ahead of his slime!

Foul owls fool vile fowls.

Birds called "fulmars" defend themselves by spray-vomiting orange stomach oil. Not surprisingly, it smells awful.

AND THAT'S WHY YOU'RE NOT GETTING A PET FULMAR.

Galactic ticks tickle tikes.

Muskrats
wax Max's 'stache.

The maggots of the human botfly burrow under your skin and live there for five to twelve weeks. When fly maggots infest your body, it's called "myiasis."

IT'S ALSO CALLED "REALLY DISGUSTING."

Tapeworms are parasites that live in your intestines. They can grow up to 82 feet long and live for 30 years.

ON THE PLUS SIDE, YOU'LL ALWAYS HAVE PLENTY OF BAIT!

Big bedbugs bite pet pugs' butts.

What's the grossest musical instrument?

WHY ARE YOU ASKING ME THIS?!

A puke-ulele!

Splat!
The fat rat is flat.

Wretched Riddles

What lives in Australia,
jumps, and smells terrible?

A KANGA-POO.

Who has round ears, speaks
in a high voice, and is gross?

ICKY MOUSE.

How do you know a
scorpion is going to fart?

*SHE ASKS YOU TO PULL
HER STINGER.*

Does a sick dog bark or arf?
NEITHER—HE BARFS.

Who lives in the woods,
loves honey, and
sticks to everything?
WINNIE-THE-GOO.

How did the leech cross the ocean?
IN A BLOOD VESSEL.

Who breathes fire and
loves infection?
PUS THE MAGIC DRAGON.

Why did the dung beetle
smear poop on his head?
*HE WANTED TO PUT
ON HIS THINKING CRAP.*

What's inside a cow's nose?
MOO-CUS.

Why did the road avoid the chicken?
BECAUSE SHE WAS FOUL.

Sis, **kiss** this **squished** **squid!**

When attacked, hagfish produce a big bucket's worth of slime in half a second.

BUT THEY ALMOST NEVER POST VIDEOS TO YOUTUBE.

To ward off predators, horned lizards can shoot foul-tasting blood out of their eyes, as far as six feet.

BUT THEN, WHY WOULD YOU WANT TO EAT A HORNED LIZARD, ANYWAY?

27

Wheezy weevils and evil weasels.

Baby Booger, why wouldn't anyone kiss the chef?

It was against restaurant policy!

He had really bad broth.

Gross **cows** grease **cross** geese.

Fussy, funky, fuzzy fungus.

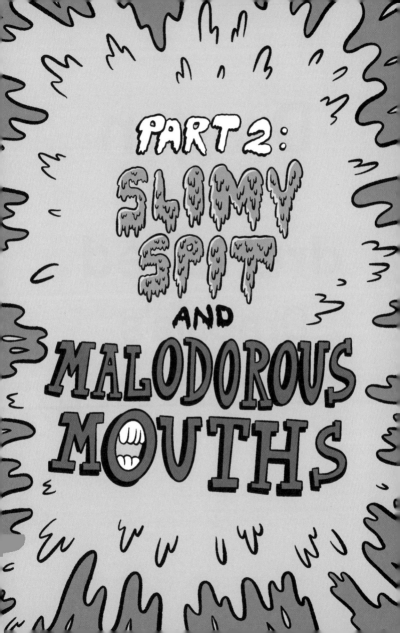

Dragon
drool
drenched
Dracula's
dragster.

Silvia slathers saliva slivers on silver.

Sing a funk song of tongue fungus tongs!

Lila's saliva's alive.

Bud's taste buds taste bugs.

Brandon's breath broke Brenda's brain.

Cows burp and fart 30 to 50 gallons of gas a day.

*IF THEY DIDN'T, WOULD THE SKY
BE FULL OF FLOATING COWS?*

Female mosquitoes don't bite with teeth.

"WHEW."

They stab your skin with six mouthparts that are like needles.

"AAAAAHHH!"

This is a book of tongue twisters, right?

Right...?

So how about some TONGUE RIDDLES

How about not.

When is a tongue like a dog's tail?

Ugh.

When it's furry?

Are the bumps on your tongue friends?

Maybe.

When it wags!

Yeah, they're buds.

Why did the ice cream cone give up?

He was melting?

He knew when he'd been licked.

40

What do tongues say on Halloween? "Happy Halloween?"

"Lick or treat!"

I think that's enough riddles about tongues, Bigger Booger.

What's even grosser than a gross tongue twister?

Two gross tongue twisters?

A dung twister. I can see that.

When is a sentence like a tornado?

What will you get if you try to say too many twisters?

Are you done?

When it blows you away?

This book?

When it's a twister!

A tongue-y ache.

For now.

Bert burped burnt bird burgers.

Ghouly Julie's truly drooly.

Chuck
upchucks
chipmunk
chunks.

After eating a course of raw salmon
with caviar at a banquet, President
George H. W. Bush vomited on the
Japanese prime minister's pants.

BUT THE BAND DID NOT PLAY
"HURL TO THE CHIEF."

Slobbering zombies slumbering soundly.

Drooling
Drew
draws duel
tools.

In your lifetime, you'll produce about 94 bathtubs of spit.

IF ONLY YOUR MOUTH COULD MAKE SOAP, TOO.

To cure bad breath, one ancient Roman philosopher recommended rubbing your teeth with honey and burnt mouse dung ashes.

"HURRY UP, MOUSE—I'VE GOT A BIG DATE TONIGHT!"

Flying phlegm flusters flutists.

We're back! What's the best game to play in a garbage dump?

Hide-and-reek!

Glad grads gulp gravy globs.

Why do you have to be brave to make kidney and liver pie?

Because it's super gross?

It takes a lot of guts.

BOO!

True Tongue-Twister Tidbits

What's the hardest tongue twister?

A researcher at the Massachusetts Institute of Technology came up with what she thinks could be the hardest tongue twister in English: "Pad kid poured curd pulled cod." *The good news is you'll never have to say it, because it makes no sense!*

Why are tongue twisters hard to say?

It's a little complicated. Different parts of the brain control the different parts of the tongue, mouth, and lips that create different related sounds. For example, one location in your brain is in charge of you making the "s" sound and the "sh" sound. When you try to say, "Shy Sammy sneezes sheaves of cheese" quickly, your brain can mix up "s" and "sh" because those sounds are controlled by the same brain area. There may be other causes of the tongue-twister effect, and scientists are still learning them. *Fanks for ashking.*

Do other languages besides English have tongue twisters?

Many do. For example, there's a famous Spanish tongue twister that goes *"Tres tristes tigres tragaban trigo en un trigal."* It means "Three sad tigers swallowed wheat in a wheat field." One in Swahili is *"Haraka haraka haina baraka,"* which means "Hurry, hurry, has no blessing." *Now you can mess up in more languages!*

Are there tongue twisters in sign language?

Yes! Combinations of words that are tricky to sign in American Sign Language are called "finger fumblers." "Good blood, bad blood," for example, is hard to sign. *And it's not that easy to say, either.*

What was the first tongue twister?

No one really knows. But hard-to-say sentences have been around for centuries, sometimes used for practicing good pronunciation. We do know that the term first became popular around 1895. One of the earliest phrases to be called a tongue twister was "Miss Smith's fish-sauce shop." *Hopefully her sauce wasn't slop.*

Bonus fact!

Scientists have discovered that even reading tongue twisters *silently* can slow down a reader. *This book may take longer than you thought to finish!*

Bedbug breath bothers Brett's brother Bronsen.

That growling in your stomach is called "borborygmus." It's caused by gas and fluid moving through your intestines.

NOT BY BEARS.

Scientists have found over 600 kinds of bacteria in human mouths.

NOW THAT'S A VARIED DIET!

Barf-breathed buddies best be bachelors.

Phil films phlegm.

Looks like Luke likes rook* licks.

* A rook is a crow-like bird.

PART 3:
PUTRID
PEOPLE
AND
ICKY
INDIVIDUALS

Grandma Gladys grips her glass of greasy gristle.

The glands that pump out skin oil are most heavily concentrated on your scalp and face, which is why you get zits and greasy hair.

OH, THANKS A LOT, NATURE!

In eighteenth-century England, people ate viper soup.

SOUNDS DELISH-HISS.

She sings sushi shanties.

Hey, Baby Booger, what's so gross about charging a battery?

I...don't...know.

It's re-volting.

Tangy toenail trimmings tempt Tony.

Hal's toe cyst has halitosis.*

*bad breath

Twist Level

4

Professional pimple popping produces plentiful pus.

Forty
farting
founding
fathers.

For hundreds of years, people consumed slain gladiators' blood and livers to cure their epilepsy.

THIS EXPLAINS THE RARITY OF EPILEPTIC VAMPIRES.

Hippocrates, a doctor in ancient Greece who's often called the father of medicine, tasted his patients' earwax.

NOW THAT'S DEDICATION!

Wretched Riddles

Which Pokémon has the
weakest stomach?

PIKA-SPEW.

Which artist only
painted with yellow?

PABLO PEE-CASSO.

Who was America's sloppiest writer?

MARK STAIN.

Who was the bloodiest Viking?

LEECH ERIKSON.

What do you call a
piece of moldy fruit
with magical powers?
HAIRY ROTTER.

What do you call a
pimple on the guy
behind home plate?
A CATCHER'S ZIT.

Which cartoon character
is yellow, mischievous,
and nauseated?
BARF SIMPSON.

Who was the smelliest
Egyptian pharaoh?
KING BUTT.

Knock, knock. *Who's there?*
Isabel. *Isabel who?*
IS A BELCH WORSE THAN A BURP?

Who was the
grossest composer?
JOHANN SEBASTIAN BLECH.

Bob blabs 'bout swabbin' skin scabs.

Fund Fern's foot fungus funhouse!

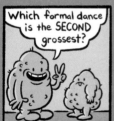

Which formal dance is the SECOND grossest?

The Slightly Less Hair Ball?

The Eye Ball.

Yeah, eyeballs are gross.

Garth's harsh barf.

Microscopic arachnids live in our eyelashes. These tiny wormlike mites have stubby legs with claws.

WORST OF ALL, THEY PAY NO RENT!

Explain spleens, please.

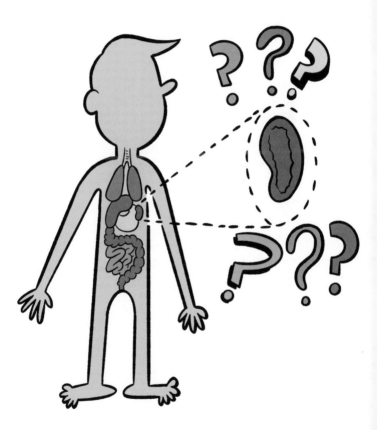

Santa feeds centipedes.

In 2012, a woman went to the hospital after five days with an itchy ear. Doctors found a spider living in her ear and flushed it out with saltwater.

EVEN PETER PARKER WAS GROSSED OUT.

When they ran out of food on their trip around the world, Ferdinand Magellan's crew ate ox hides and rats.

"I SMELL A RAT . . . YUM!"

Candace can't stand Stan's stench.

What do you say to year-old vomit?

"Please leave?"

"Happy Barf Day!"

Please leave.

Miss Moss's moth misses math.

Ask a Pile of Rotting Garbage

Hello, dear readers. I may be a pile of rotting garbage, but I am a *highly educated* pile of rotting garbage. So let's hear your questions about the whys and wherefores of disgust!

Dear Pile of Rotting Garbage,
What happens to our bodies when we are grossed out?

Gagging in Glasgow

Dear Gagging,
When something really grosses you out (like a pile of rotting garbage), your blood pressure drops, you start sweating, and in extreme cases you might gag—or faint. Don't worry, I won't take it personally.

● ● ●

Dear Pile of Rotting Garbage,
Why do we even get grossed out at all?

Scabby in Schenectady

Dear Scabby,
Researchers at the London School of Hygiene and Tropical Medicine say that we have a disgusted reaction to things that can make us sick—sick people, rotting food, and unclean things. So disgust is a way our bodies show us that we should avoid certain potentially harmful things. Sometimes we are grossed out by things we personally find disgusting that others do not.

✦ ■ ✦

Dear Pile of Rotting Garbage,
Why, when we are grossed out, do our faces get all squished up and we stick out our tongues?

Putrid in Pittsburgh

Dear Putrid,
Some experts think it probably has something to do with keeping potentially harmful stuff from getting in our bodies. Sticking out our tongues would push out gross stuff, and closed eyes would keep it from getting in there.

✦ ■ ✦

Dear Pile of Rotting Garbage,
When I see someone throw up, why do I feel like hurling, too?

Queasy in Quebec

Dear Queasy,
Some scientists think this kind of reaction results from special nerves, called "mirror neurons," that make us feel the feelings that we observe in other people. There's still the question of why that guy in the *mirror* pukes at the same time as you . . .

Yaks jog on Jack's yacht.

After exercising, Romans scraped off their oil and sweat, which was collected and sold as medicine.

"YOU KNOW WHAT'LL CURE THAT? SWEATY OIL."

A California scientist used bacteria from human feet and armpits to make cheese.

BUT ISN'T THAT CANNIBALISM?

Twist Level **3**.

Insects
in socks
incense
ensigns.*

*a low-ranking Navy officer. Pronounced "en-sin."

Why didn't the gooey mass get hired?

He wasn't qualified?

He failed the blob interview.

Squid squads squirt square dancers.

What did the skin say to the cut?

"Hi, cut?"

"You look scab-ulous!"

Ick.

Fred feeds three freed flies fries.

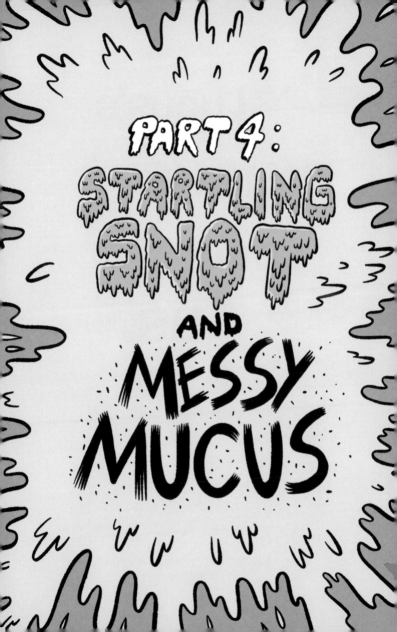

PART 4:
STARTLING
SNOT
AND
MESSY
MUCUS

Lucus's
mucus
spooks
us.

There's a kind of jellyfish that can launch balls of mucus filled with stinging cells.

SAY NO TO PLAYING "CATCH" WITH THOSE GUYS.

Your nose and throat produce one to two quarts of mucus every day.

S'NOT BAD.

No niece's nice nose needs a nasty nasal nest.

Hey, Baby Booger, what's the best weapon for germ warfare?

I suppose "germs" is too obvious.

A phlegm-thrower.

Sue's **snoot** is Stu's **suit.**

Burglars burgle beagle boogers.

Ross got lost in the boss's proboscis.*

*nose

The scientific term for picking your nose too much is "rhinotillexomania."

ARE YOU A RHINOTILLEXOMANIAC?

89

Big
pigs pick
snout
snot.

After a backpacking trip in 2014, a woman found a three-inch leech living in her nose. She named it Mr. Curly but had doctors remove it.

THE BEST PART OF TRAVEL: MAKING NEW FRIENDS.

The speeds of sneezes have been measured up to 100 miles per hour—shooting out as many as 100,000 contagious germs.

THAT'S A LOT OF SPEEDING TICKETS.

Definitions of Frequently Used Gross Words

Use this handy guide and you'll finally be able to tell a blob from a glob!

Know Your Nose Goo

Booger: An individual piece of dried nasal mucus

Mucus: The slimy stuff found in noses and in other parts of the body

Phlegm (pronounced "flem"): Excess mucus you get when you're sick

Snot: Nasal mucus, whether it's dry and crusty, or still moist

Gross Liquids

Goo: Sticky or thick liquid

Ooze: Slimy stuff at the bottom of a body of water or in a wet area; also, something slimy that moves slowly

Slime: A moist, jellylike substance

Hunks of Yuck

Blob: A small drop or lump of a thick liquid; a spot of color; something not well defined, amorphous

Glob: A small drop; a large and rounded mass

Gob: A lump; a large amount of something

Lump: A mass of indefinite shape

Sludge: Muddy stuff; gunk left over from sewage treatment and other processes

Miscellaneous Ick

Bile: Yellow or green liquid created by your liver

Gunk: Dirty, greasy, or sticky stuff

Mush: Thick porridge or something soft, spongey, and shapeless

Pus: Thick, yellowish-white liquid that often forms around an infection

He sees Steve and his knees sneeze.

How do you start a booger race?

Oh! I don't know.

Ready, set... BLOW!

Cousin Ronald cuddles nasal noodles.

Bigger boogers boggle bagel baggers.

Mucus is actually useful for fighting infections, so some scientists are trying to create artificial snot!

MY NOSE MAKES MEDICINE?

Your Highness, your sinus! No dryness— a two-ply mess.

Sniffling suggests secret snot supplies.

Monkeys and apes have been observed in the wild using sticks and grass to pick their noses.

LUCKY FOR THEM THERE ARE A LOT OF STICKS IN THE WILD.

Doctors helped out a man with a drippy nostril by removing a tooth that had grown inside his nasal cavity.

THAT EXPLAINS THE BITE MARKS ON HIS FOREFINGER.

Prospector Penelope picked her possum's proboscis.

How did the kid win his first gross contest?

Hard work?

Beginner's yuck.

Sheila seizes Celia's sneezy schnozz.

The Twister Bowl

Compete against a friend for some tongue-tying, mouth-mangling matches!

Endurance Run

The ultimate face-off! You and a friend each choose any tongue twister. Then take turns trying to say that twister as many times as possible within twenty seconds without messing up. Count the total number of correctly recited twisters for each competitor. In case of a draw, use this twister for a tie-breaker round:

"If it's a tie, try Ty's tie tea."

Say It, Don't Spray It!

Hold a piece of paper close to your mouth as you say this twister ten times fast:

> "Theda Thorn thought three thousand thoughts and theories."

Have a friend do the same. Which of you got less spit on the paper? The less-moist talker wins!

Hop and Don't Stop

While each hopping on one foot, you and a friend must try to repeat:

> "Hairless Harry hopped halfway to Halifax, happily hurling halibuts."

The first one to mess up the twister or to stop hopping on one foot is the loser.

Slow and Steady

Using a timer or stopwatch, see how slowly you and a friend can each say:

> "Slow Joe rowed to Flo."

The tricky part is that you can only take a breath between words, so for maximum slow, you'll have to strreeeeeeetch each word out. The longest time wins!

Not Scott's snot!

Hawaiian monk seals sometimes get eels stuck in their noses.

MAYBE PASTA WOULD BE A SAFER MEAL?

The parrotfish sleeps in a sack of its own mucus.

THAT'S ONE SLIMY SLEEPING BAG.

Mose's nose is Rose's hose.

Snot

rockets

rot

sprocket

sockets.

Why did the people pick a baby as their king?

Oh, I know! Because babies RULE!

No, they thought he would make a good drooler. That's pretty much what I said.

Nasal nuggets need nightly nourishment.

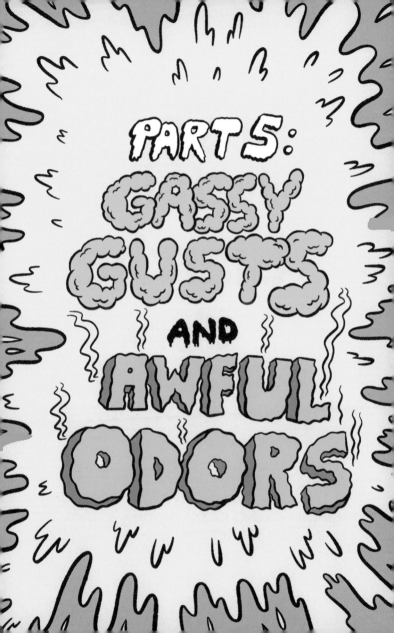

Terry's daily dairy diarrhea diary.

During the hot summer of 1858, sewage in London's Thames River gave off such a terrible smell that it became known as the "Great Stink."

THIS HAS NOTHING TO DO WITH YOUR FEET.

Sweat doesn't really smell bad. It's the bacteria that live in your armpits and other sweaty places that do the stinking.

WE CAN STILL CALL IT B.O., THOUGH.

Bart farts.

Art barfs.

Flames
frighten
flatulent
Frenchmen.

Rotten Reg rubs **eggs** on legs.

Pity Patty's porta-potty pottery.

Scientists say Uranus smells terrible. They've detected hydrogen sulfide in its clouds, the gas that makes rotten eggs stink.

WHOEVER NAMED THAT PLANET JUST HAD A HUNCH . . .

115

Battle bots betrayed by binary butt blasts!

Archaeologists in Texas found a 1,500-year-old piece of fossilized human poop with snake bones, scales, and a fang in it. They concluded that someone ate a whole venomous viper.

"WAITER, THERE'S A FANG IN MY SNAKE . . ."

In the 1890s, Joseph Pujol starred as Le Pétomane in Paris's Moulin Rouge nightclub. He imitated animals and performed the French national anthem . . . with farts.

EVEN AT ITS BEST, HIS ACT STANK.

This tongue twister isn't gross as written, but try saying it quickly and it will undergo an odorous transformation . . .

One smart fellow, he felt smart. Two smart fellows,

Which sea is the grossest?

The Dead Sea?

The Nausea.

Hmm. Only works in print.

they felt
smart.
Three smart
fellows, they
all felt
smart.

Pete's poots pollute Polly's pool party.

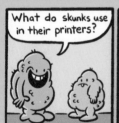

Gassy germs gobble jerky.

Pappy's pups peep porpoise poop.

During his reign as the king of England, Henry VIII had four Grooms of the Stool in charge of the royal toilet, all of them knights.

THEY WORKED THEIR WAY UP FROM THE BOTTOM.

Self-sulfuring surfers suffer.

Doug's tongue dug dung.

The earliest known joke was a fart joke recorded in Sumeria in 1900 BCE.

IT HAS WAFTED THROUGH THE AGES.

People pass gas an average of 14 to 22 times a day.

THAT'S A LOT OF FINGER PULLING!

Sora's sour sewer shower.

What's the difference between a toilet and a towelette?

I don't know.

Then remind me to never ask you for a towelette.

Guzzling gutter gunk guarantees gurgling gas.

Why did the man's fart go "ha ha ha"?

Please don't ask me that.

He had a bad case of laughing gas.

Help.

Knock-Knock (on the Bathroom Door) Jokes

Knock, knock!
Who's there?
Harry.
Harry who?
Harry up! I need to use the bathroom.

Knock, knock!
Who's there?
O'Reilly.
O'Reilly who?
O'Reilly gotta go!

Knock, knock!
Who's there?
Hope.
Hope who?
Hope you're not stinking up the place!

· · ·

Knock, knock!
Who's there?
Lotta.
Lotta who?
Lotta people out here waiting!

· · ·

Knock, knock!
Who's there?
Donna.
Donna who?
Donna forget to wash your hands.

· · ·

Knock, knock!
Who's there?
Stan.
Stan who?
Stan back, I'm gonna break down this door!

Behold:
B.O.
bingo!

Baby koalas eat their moms' poop.

NOT CUTE.

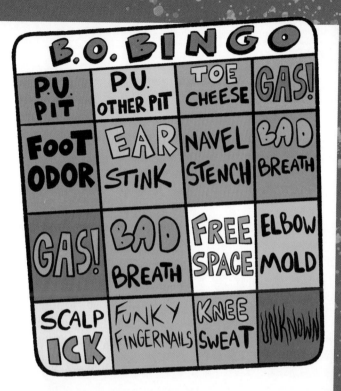

Groups of rhinos pick one spot to poop on. (It can be 65 feet across.) Then they sniff the chemicals in the dung to learn information about one another.

THEY REALLY NEED FACEBOOK.

Commode commandos command common courtesy.

Which dessert comes with whipped cream, cherries, and drool?

One you send back?

A banana spit.

The flatulent lieutenant resents his ten-cent tent's scent.

Who was the smelliest French general?

I don't know any French generals.

Napoleon Blow-a-Fart.

Tot totes toy toilet.

Toad Lou's tofu is toe goo.

Toe jam can be composed of dead skin, sweat, dirt, fabric from clothes, bacteria, and fungus.

I DON'T WANT TO JAM WITH THAT BAND.

The corpse flower has big, beautiful blooms. Unfortunately, they stink like rotting meat.

NOT SUITABLE FOR MOTHER'S DAY.

Pip pops zits.

Pop zaps pots.

Tanning tonsils turn tongues tingly.

How do you know when a dinosaur poops on your car?

Yuck! I have no idea, Bigger Booger.

The windshield wipers won't work.

Urk!

PLOP

Earwax in packs are snacks.

Autumn orders odder otter odors.

The strings of violins, harps, guitars, banjos, and other stringed instruments are often made from animal intestines.

THAT EXPLAINS WHY SOME PEOPLE'S PLAYING SOUNDS LIKE A DYING CHICKEN.

Gert's goat's got guts.

A goat's first stomach (they have four) can hold five whole gallons of chewed plants. The result is a lot of gas, so goats do a lot of burping.

TRY TO BLEAT THAT!

A 3,000-year-old mummy in Peru was found with 545 lice on its head.

WERE THEY WRAPPED IN TINY LITTLE BANDAGES?

Short but Deadly

"Toy boat" is a famous, short tongue twister that doesn't look like it should trip up anyone's tongue. But try saying it ten times fast. Did you notice that you ended up making mistakes with vowel sounds in one or both words?

Some scientists believe that "toy boat" is hard to say because your tongue has to move positions very quickly. Saying "toy" makes the middle of your tongue touch the

What's the grossest bath toy?

A really old one?

A rubber yucky.

roof of your mouth. Your tongue needs to move down quickly to say "boat"—and this may be too much action for your tongue, especially if you have to speak quickly.

It's also possible that English speakers' brains are just not used to vowels and consonants in this particular combination, and that's why "toy boat" starts to come out as "tuh but" or "toy boyt" after many repetitions.

Here are some other two-word tongue twisters that don't look hard . . . but watch out! They are double trouble!

Thin thing

French friend

Smart fart

Top cop

Big whip

Soy poot

Tapeworms take turns tasting Vern.

Brad's bread bled bloodred.

How did the slime creature do on her report card?

Slimily?

She got straight ooze. That makes sense.

Charles's chaps chafe chapped cheeks.

A type of ocean worm that lives off the coast of Scotland has a pair of eyes on its butt.

FULL-TIME REARVIEW!

Plush
bus
plus
pus.

Puke pails pour plentifully, painting Paul's Porsche.

Researchers in North Carolina have built a vomiting machine, which aids them in studying a virus that causes throwing up.

A VOMITING MACHINE?
CALL IT THE GERMINATOR, I GUESS.

For hundreds of years up until the 1960s, there was a color of paint called "Mummy brown" that was made from actual ground-up Egyptian mummies.

TOMB IT MAY CONCERN: THIS WAS A BAD IDEA!

Six sick psychics itch stitches.

Which football team is full of pus?

I don't want to think about that.

The Buffalo Boils.

Wrestling wallabies whistle wretchedly.

How did the cops catch the Alphabet Thief?

Good, solid forensic evidence?

He stopped to take a P.

Ouch.

Dare to Twist

If you're feeling brave (or weird), try these ideas for some strange tongue-twister stunts.

Befuddle a friend by texting them an unannounced random tongue twister!

Do you enjoy attempting to telepathically communicate with pets? Try breaking the ice by sending them your favorite tongue twister by thinking at them!

The next time a parent asks you a question, reply with your favorite tongue twister!

Singing in the shower is for poseurs! Instead, entertain yourself by yelling out your favorite tongue twisters while showering!

Baffle video game teammates by saying your favorite tongue twisters via your headset during heated gameplay.

When called on in class, answer your teacher's question with a tongue twister! (Only do this if your teacher is in a good mood.)

Set up a lemonade stand and offer "One Free Tongue Twister with Each Lemonade Drink!"

The next time your mouth is frozen and numb from icy-beverage consumption, try to say some tongue twisters.

Make a fake Santa beard using some shaving cream, and then attempt to say some twisters from this book!

Brit bit a zit as she knit a nit mitt.

A dirty cell phone can cause acne breakouts.

STANDARD PIMPLE-POPPING RATES APPLY.

Slugs can use their own slime trail to find their way home.

FOLLOW THE YUCKY ICK ROAD.

Cracked crickets crank-call creek crocs.

Who was the smelliest Egyptian queen?

I can't even guess.

B-O-patra.

Sid sips Seth's sixth soaked sock.

Slugs chug mugs of sludge.

160

Watch cats wash Sasquatch.

Since 1976, the FBI has had a file on Bigfoot (aka Sasquatch).

DO THEY KNOW HIS SHOE SIZE?

The Apex Regional Landfill about an hour north of Las Vegas is America's biggest dump. It covers 2,200 acres and holds over 50 million tons of garbage.

WHAT A DUMP!

White whales write wretched rock 'n' roll.

Ghost goats goad ghouls.

Hey, Baby Booger! What's putrid and sings?

A singer with no talent?

A zombie doing karaoke.

Beasts boast: "Best boats!"

Which witches wash which watches?

In an English cave, archaeologists have found 14,700-year-old human skulls shaped into cups or bowls.

THAT'S USING YOUR HEAD . . . OR SOMEONE ELSE'S.

Lagoon lurkers like leaky lifeboats.

Which Jedi knight has the weakest stomach?

I'm stumped, Bigger Booger.

PUKE SKYWALKER

Gross Monster Facts

The facts are all real, even if some of the creatures mentioned aren't.

Bigfoot

People who claim to have seen Bigfoot, or Sasquatch, say that the creature gives off a scent like rotting meat or horse poop. *Maybe his big foot stepped in something?*

Hungry Ghosts

In Chinese traditional beliefs, there are types of spirits called "Hungry Ghosts." One Hungry Ghost pukes fire, another eats pus, and one is made completely out of putrid hair! *Instead of "eek," these ghosts make you go "ick!"*

Mummies

When the bodies of many ancient Egyptians were mummified, the brains were pulled out through the corpses' noses with a special tool. In 2012, archaeologists discovered that one of those tools had been left in a 2,400-year-old corpse by a careless embalmer. *Nice work, brainless!*

Godzilla

The actor who played Godzilla in films from 1954 to 1973 got so hot inside the rubber suit he wore as the monster that he could wring out half a bucket of sweat from his undershirt after filming. *Monster work is thirsty work.*

Dinosaurs

Mining fossilized dinosaur poop was big business in England in the 1800s. It could be used as fertilizer. *Eat your potatoes, kids—they're grown with dino-poop!*

Giant Squid

A giant squid's esophagus (the tube where food travels from beak to stomach) passes through a hole in the animal's brain. So they have to take small bites or risk brain damage. *Giant squid, small portions.*

The Bonnacon

In the Middle Ages, people in Europe heard tales of a legendary beast called the "Bonnacon," which was said to have the body of a bull, the mane of a horse, and curved horns. It supposedly would defend itself by shooting out blasts of burning dung! *The best defense is a good offensive smell!*

Akaname

Japanese folklore tradition includes bothersome spirits called "Yokai." Some of them are pretty gross, like the Akaname—little men with long tongues who haunt bathrooms and lick the grime off wooden bathtubs. *Useful but revolting.*

Mumbling numb mummies.

Marcia must mix Martian marsh mush.

Pat's
bad
bat
bath.

Though they drink blood, vampire bats can also be cuddly and oftentimes groom one another.

JUST WATCH IT WITH THOSE FANGS, PAL!

Hairy hearing holes horrify hordes.

Bats bite bots' butts.

Cities around the world are beginning to use robots to inspect and unclog their sewer systems.

BEEP BOOP. PLOP PLOP.

Some piranhas are vegetarians.

THEY STILL WON'T EAT TOFU, THOUGH.

Moon men mainly maintain monsters.

Overeager ogre eater.

What did the slobby train conductor have on his shirt?

A logo for some company?

A chew-chew stain.

Yuck.

Wretched Riddles

What's 400 feet tall and
full of slimy pulp?

GOURD-ZILLA.

Why do vampires love tic-tac-toe?

BECAUSE X MARKS THE CLOT.

Who's huge and hairy
with tiny underpants?

KING THONG.

Why do baby zombies
throw so many tantrums?

THEY'RE SPOILED ROTTEN.

Why do T. rexes take
so long in the bathroom?

*THEIR ARMS ARE TOO
SHORT TO WIPE WITH.*

Who walks upright, hides
in the woods, and is always
stepping on insects?

BUG-FOOT.

What's the fastest setting
on a witch's broom?

WART SPEED.

Who lives in a Scottish
lake and loves the
taste of garbage?

THE LICK MESS MONSTER.

What's inside a ghost's nose?

BOO-GERS.

What did Dr. Jekyll turn
into when he drank
electric eel blood?

MR. FRIED.

A goblin's job is gobblin' gobs.

In Mexico, there are folktales about a kind of goblin called a "duende," which lives in the bedroom walls of children and tries to clip their toenails.

CREEPY . . . BUT SORT OF HELPFUL.

Scientists have proposed that the Loch Ness monster may be a giant eel and not a dinosaur-era aquatic lizard.

CONGRATULATIONS, SCIENTISTS, FOR MAKING IT JUST AS SCARY!

Newly nuclear newts nuke nudists.

When is a booger not a booger?

No idea.

When it's not.
Oh, "snot." I see. Classic!

Mark makes snake-pit snacks.

Her raptor wrapped her **rat.**

A large barge is lodged in Marge's schnozz.

A quarter teaspoon of saliva can have over 200 billion bacteria in it.

MAYBE YOU SHOULD REGISTER YOUR SPIT AS A LETHAL WEAPON.

There's a kind of fungus that can take over an ant's brain and control it.

THAT'S NO PICNIC!

Nasal fossils are awful waffles.

What did the hagfish say when he fooled the leech?

I don't think fish can talk.

"Sucker!" Blech.

Dan's **rough** on Dean's **dandruff.**

Dapper diapered divers.

Otto ought to automate outhouses.

A champion eater set a world record when he ate 141 hard-boiled eggs in eight minutes.

EGG-SHELL-ENT!

Tornado tasting typifies teenaged tomfoolery.

Hey, Bigger Booger! What's the smelliest constellation?

What did you—?

The Big Diaper!

Which fish is the grossest?

I ask the questions around—

The hali-BUTT!

Gross-Out
Fake-Out

The bold words below may appear disgusting but they really aren't. The real definitions are upside down beneath the words.

Bumfuzzle doesn't mean to grow thick fur on your rear end. It means . . .

TO CONFUSE.

A **buttress** isn't a fortress made out of human buttocks. It's . . .

SOMETHING THAT SUPPORTS.

Fanny-blower isn't a word for a new invention that wafts farts far away. It's . . .

A NINETEENTH-CENTURY TERM FOR AN INDUSTRIAL FAN.

A **fartlek** isn't an animal that smells flatulence with its tongue. It's . . .

A TYPE OF TRAINING THAT INVOLVES FAST RUNNING MIXED WITH SLOW RUNNING.

Fleech doesn't describe the action of a runaway leech. It means . . .

TO ENCOURAGE BY MEANS OF FLATTERY.

Fungible isn't a word for people who like mushrooms. It means . . .

INTERCHANGEABLE OR FLEXIBLE.

Mundungus isn't a kind of manure you use on Mondays. It's . . .

BAD-SMELLING TOBACCO.

Nincompoop is not something you find in a toilet. It's . . .

A FOOLISH OR STUPID PERSON.

Nudibranch isn't a government agency for people who like to go without clothes. It's . . .

A COLORFUL, SLUGLIKE MARINE ANIMAL.

To **scabble** doesn't mean to collect scabs. It means . . .

TO ROUGHLY SHAPE.

No
hares
share
nose
hair.

Which playing card stinks the worst?

I don't like this! You can't —

The Ace of Farts!

Madge's magnet got maggots in Natchez.

Poodles

paddle

piddle

puddles.

No one really knows why dogs roll in smelly stuff, but most experts agree that, to dogs, the odors smell good.

I NEVER GO OUT WITHOUT A QUICK SPRITZ OF ROTTING-FISH PERFUME!

An English organization studying pet nutrition created a special suit for canines to help researchers collect and study dog farts.

THAT'S THE EASY PART. LOOKING AT FARTS UNDER A MICROSCOPE IS MUCH HARDER.

Slow cop, go plow cow plop.

204

Mosquitoes most miss moist musk.

Why did the driver stomp on his fart?

Stop it!

He wanted to step on the gas!
GASP!

Stu spewed stewed foods.

Surgeons sometimes put maggots *into* wounds. The wormy fly larvae can actually help get rid of dead tissue by eating it.

WHAT'S ON THE MENU TONIGHT? YOU ARE!